Being Informed

By Dr. Kendall Johnson, Ed.D,
LCSW, LMSW, MSW, BSW,
NCCE, NCPC, MAC, CFTP,
NCDVC,
FVIP, SAP, EMDR Trained

Publishing Company: Success for Family and Children Enterprise Publishing
463 Pooler Parkway #112
Pooler, GA. 31322
912-323-9784
Email-successforfandc@aol.com
ISBN: 9798868979200

Acknowledgements

This book is written with special acknowledgement to my husband, son, my godmother, family members, friends, and mentors. I would also like to acknowledge my parents and brother who are deceased and my dear Luke who recently passed away.

Thank you all for the encouragement and support throughout life, and thank you to those who waited patiently for the book to be written. I love and appreciate each of you!

Dr. Kendall Johnson

Disclaimer

Information in this book is for educational purposes, to help individuals learn about resources so that they can better advocate for themselves and make the necessary changes to lessen stressors. Services mentioned vary from state to state and business to business. What is currently available in one area may not be available in another area or may have never been available. Next, eligibility criteria for services tend to be updated on an ongoing basis and should be verified as one seeks assistance.

Interviews were completed with individuals who experienced the situations mentioned in the book and with professionals and experts who verified or confirmed information listed in this informational text. Public announcements were also found on the internet regarding some of the topics. If a service is no longer available or was not available in a local area or state, do not be alarmed. Stay encouraged, and understand that changes occur on a regular basis.

Table of Contents

Preface

This book is long overdue. Working in the profession of social work for over 40 years, it warms my heart to help individuals learn ways to reduce stressors. Everyone has tools that they use to get through life events or else one would wonder, how do individuals survive?

Working in various settings and with diverse groups, I witnessed and heard about levels of stress that contributed to major health issues, the

breaking up of family units,
employment losses, and death.

In one way, stress can be looked at as a silent killer. It contributes to the development or worsening of mental, psychological, and emotional sicknesses and illnesses. Stress can also initiate or increase drug and alcohol abuse, anxiety, depression, panic attacks, as well as thoughts and acts of suicide. Individuals may also experience body pains, headaches, and hair loss.

This emotion of stress can also cause individuals to experience sleepless nights, changes in vision and eating habits, heart attacks, eating disorders, financial hardships, and some violent behaviors.

I work with individuals whose levels of stress also impede or hinder them from pursuing and accomplishing life goals and objectives. Stress impacts their self-esteem as well. This emotion is so powerful that if one lacks healthy coping skills or does not have proper support systems or lacks resources, they are headed for some serious, lifelong challenges.

Because of the power of stress, many people fake how they present themselves and how they live out their life cycle. People smile, laugh, and tell others that they are doing well when they are hiding the truth. Telling the truth means pulling off our armors and shields, expressing our true emotions, whatever those emotions are. Others will find out that a person is not who they want others to think that they are or doing as well as they want others to believe that they are. I must admit that I have been in this state of mind many times before I learned to ask questions, ask for help, and document information explained to me so I can become and remain informed.

Shields and Armors

I am amazed regarding the many shields and armors used privately and in public because of the feelings of stress. Shields and armors are thrown in the corners of rooms, not to be touched until the next outside appearance. They are retrieved when it is necessary to cover secrets of who someone really is or to describe what and how they are doing mentally and/or physically.

Life Changes

Nothing is meant to remain the same in life. Change is necessary for growth and is part of human development. This is challenging because it means getting out of your comfort zone to go into an area that is unknown. One is challenged to develop the necessary coping skills to make changes in the healthiest ways, or negative outcomes can result.

Not all stress is unhealthy. One can learn from outcomes to help with future growth or better decision-making. Stress is healthy when it does not monopolize or impact someone to the point that they are unable to focus for extended periods of time or unable to gain or regain a level of healthy calmness. Trust me; drug abuse, alcohol abuse, verbal abuse, and violence in any form is not the answer to resolving issues.

I must admit that my life has not been without major stressors. If it was not for my support systems, role assignments, and the morals and values of which remain with me, my life would undoubtedly be different. Many of my successes would have been delayed, and my mental health would have been greatly challenged.

A few of my life stressors at an early age, includes a brother being killed drag racing and the death of close family members within months apart due to health issues. My mother kept me close for our mental stability. I was truly blessed to have an active and supportive father and stepfather in my life. My mother entrusted family members, friends, neighbors, church members, and other positive people in our lives for spiritual and life balances. My family system was extended to include many.

In the community, my family had a very positive image, so my support teams were sometimes overwhelming. There were not many places or things that I could do where someone in my system wouldn't find out and correct my wrongs. Fortunately for me, they also supported and encouraged my rights.

I could say that I have a few close friends and many associates. My close friends and I have known one another for years. We laugh, cry, pray together, encourage one another, and share resources. Within our group, there is honesty and sensitivity to feelings and emotions. In the circle, I have the title and role of the social worker/therapist. When we are out, someone will start a pleasant conversation with me or with my friends, and I always find myself sharing meaningful information.

I am grateful as I reflect on my life for the positive support that I have had over the years and fortunately still have. I know that because of the information mentioned, this is the reason that the profession of social work was my choice. While family members were and are teachers, nurses, childcare workers, pharmacists, bankers, secretaries, business owners, healthcare workers, military veterans, caretakers, etc., I am the only family member in the profession of social work.

I was raised with the saying and belief that "it takes a village to raise children." It is my belief as well that the village must support the villagers and keep their influence as encouraging as possible.

Understand that the village can offer much, but it is the responsibility of the people to make the necessary changes in their lives so that things are better or healthier for them. This is done with the need of support from multiple systems, and it is not easy.

For changes to be considered, it involves maturity, patience, the willingness to ask questions, taking advantage of available resources, and following through with what needs to be done in a timely manner. Making changes means taking risks with the unknown, which is a major stressor for many. It is sometimes believed that staying with the familiar is better when the results have not been the most favorable. What have you been taught?

The mere idea of change means there might be rejections along the way, but giving up only hinders the growth process. I learned from my systems that setting goals and timeframes helps with the process of realistic achievements. There will be times that changes will be necessary along the way, but understand that the process does not end until the goal is achieved. Giving up means defeat, and I was taught that it was not an option for me, what about you?

I enjoy communicating with others and have been told that I am easy to talk with. Sharing beliefs for encouragement and motivation is enjoyable for me, but I am very careful not to impose my beliefs or the knowledge I've gained on others because it is with respectful understanding that everyone's life journey is their own.

As mentioned, I have worked in several settings and with diverse groups of all ages, so I have heard, seen, and personally experienced a lot. There were nights that I did not sleep because of these experiences. I learned over time the true importance of having multiple support systems and self-care.

Individuals of all statuses have communicated with me via phone, emails, face-to-face, and texts, and I have gone with them as a member of their support system to help advocate for services. After all, people are people first before titles, and system support is needed by all.

With the roles and duties that I perform, I must say that I enjoy being the vessel of support to many with their shields and armors in position of protection. These mechanisms protect who people are and what is going on in their lives. I say again: the stress that is carried can be a silent killer; mentally, emotionally, psychologically, and physically.

Medical Setting

I proudly identify myself as one working in the social work profession. The settings of which someone works and the consumers who are served are key to why some possess greater knowledge than others regarding resources. In best practice, social workers are encouraged to learn as much as possible regarding local and national resources due to the diverse groups of which we work with, and the stressors that decrease with assistance.

I have worked in several settings and enjoyed them all, but one stands out more than all the others: medical social work. Working in this position, I witnessed families at their lowest points due to sudden life changes and high levels of stress. This allowed me to know that one can be laughing one moment, and everything can change in the next moment when the individual receives a text, gets a phone call, or hears a knock at the door.

As a medical social worker, I learned that without proper resources, patients and family members experience great stress after and during incidents that bring on life changes.

I worked in the progressive care unit, trauma unit, cardiovascular care, intensive care, emergency room, surgery and other areas. These were areas where you truly had to put on your armor and shields to survive what you saw, heard, and had to be part of.

Working in these areas required me to be extremely resourceful as the job duties included transferring individuals to hospitals, facilitating nursing home placements, and transferring patients to rehabilitation, psychiatric and other facilities. Duties also included arranging transportation by ground or air medical ambulances, completing Social Security and Supplemental Social Security Income applications and other forms. I also provided grief counseling and regularly conversed with insurance companies and ordered medical equipment for patients at discharge.

Home health services were set-up as well. I worked with the risk management department on select cases and worked with law enforcement when necessary. To add, I had the responsibilities of facilitating family conferences to discuss discharge planning, the needs of patients, and went with staff as they shared medical diagnoses. I was also with families when they saw their loved ones after accidents, incidents, and when they prepared to say goodbyes as machines were turned off and their loved ones passed away.

There was also the responsibility of locating family members of individuals who came to the hospital deceased and locating family members of those who expired with no identification.

Families and patients (if a patient could) would have to make decisions that they never had to in their lifetime and make them rapidly most of the time. Some of them were in disbelief or shock that their system or unit was being disrupted temporarily or permanently.

Patients were mothers, grand-mothers, children, fathers, uncles, aunts, sons, and daughters who depended on one another to help with decision-making, paying rent, paying mortgages, paying household bills, buying groceries, helping with childcare, etc. I listened as they called on different systems for help. Some got the help they needed, and others did not. I saw tears, heard verbal abuse, and saw physical altercations. Those who appeared the strongest were ever so broken. They were unable to hide behind their armors and shields because they needed help like never before.

Being a social worker, I heard the questions asked among the family members about who was going to make the overall decisions, what was going to be the cost of medical assistance, and where was the money going to come from to pay for the placement or placements. Family members had to decide who was going to be the caretaker or caretakers of a family member now that there was a change in someone's lifestyle. What stressed many out the most was the fear of not knowing.

Most lacked information regarding community resources and how to access assistance. My answer was and will continue to be, ask questions to the appropriate individuals and leave armors and shields in their appropriate places. When help is needed, it is needed regardless of race, marital status, religion, nationality, sex, creed, or socioeconomic status.

Resources

Resources are available on all levels; locally, statewide, and nationally. Some are more plentiful than others; however, knowing how to access them is key to helping with reducing many issues. Resources change often, and what is available today might not be available later, and most definitely not in all locations. One must also consider the eligibility of services and the periods of availability which tend to change regularly.

Facility Placements

When individuals are unable to safely care for their daily living needs or themselves due to changes in mental or physical health, as a medical social worker, I was responsible for finding appropriate aftercare placement or discharge planning. This required the patient, if he or she was able, and/or family members full input and cooperation. The process was and is still very confusing, stressful, and overwhelming. In most cases, decisions must be made quickly.

When someone is admitted in a medical facility, discharge planning starts the same or next few days after admission depending on the patient's condition. When conversations regarding nursing home placements were discussed, stress levels got extremely high among patients and family members.

For nursing homes and some other placements to be successful, it requires several steps to be completed. The process is different depending on if someone is in or out-patient. If someone is seeking placement and they are doing so from home (out-patient), the admission process is done with the help of the individual's primary physician's staff along with the patient or family. The medical staff will complete the appropriate paperwork and the family usually has the responsibility of finding the placement site.

If someone is in a hospital or other facility the discharge planning staff are responsible for checking with the patient's insurance (Medicaid, Medicare, private insurance, etc) to find out if there are benefits to cover the cost of the needed placement. If there are benefits, the status of the annual deductible or deductibles and the number of days eligible for insurance payments are discussed with the patient, family, and/or legal decision maker (s). If a deductible has not been met, usually it must be paid, or payment arrangements made before many facilities will allow admission. For some, this means having immediate access to hundreds and thousands of dollars.

If someone needs extended care or more days than insurance will pay, there must be another payment source. This is usually discussed at admissions or before the last day of the approved insurance payment to the facility. During the initial days of coverage, one's income is not sought after by many facilities. After such time, the income along with other funds are due for services rendered.

If a person's income is not enough to cover expenses and there are no private funds to pay the cost, there is Nursing Home Medicaid, if it is a nursing home placement, or other benefits to possibly assist. Staff will discuss the application process and benefits with the patient and responsible payor. Even if a patient can sign him or herself into a facility, it is asked prior to admission for a responsible payor to be identified.

Admission paperwork is completed at the admitting facility, and the application for Medicaid assistance is completed by the responsible payor through the Division of Family and Children Services (DFCS) in the state of Georgia. This organization might have a different name in another state. If there is no responsible party to represent the patient, measures can be taken to secure one for this purpose.

If a person's income is more than what would make them eligible for the appropriate placement Medicaid benefit, there is what is referred to as the *spenddown* to help them meet eligibility criteria. If they meet the spenddown, benefits are awarded to help with not only the cost of care but also with eligible medications in some cases. For those who are eligible without requirements of a spenddown, they too might get assistance with placement and medication costs. Not to worry though: the placement facility and Division of Family and Children Services staff are usually on point with keeping families informed regarding eligibility limits, benefits, and changes in policies.

For those who use or receive the services discussed above and other kinds of Medicaid assistance, you may have to repay the state for monies paid out for care benefits or services. If the individual possesses properties or has specific financial resources, insurances, these items will be sought after by the state. This tends to happen when a person dies, placements change, or when specific life and/or financial changes occur. Questions about assets are discussed at the time that the service application is being completed, questioned on the benefit applications or forms, and checked regularly by appropriate staff. Staff will check the Board of Assessors, banks, and other sources for the assets of the applicant.

In some states, there might be a financial penalty for property or other assets of value if they are sold within an identified period in the name of the individual who received or who is applying for Medicaid assistance. If they are not sold within the period or assets are not valued at or above the allowed amount, there might not be a penalty. Next, if there are no resources in the person's name at death, bills might be forgiven. This is the term that I use for no repayment. Refer to the Medicaid Recovery Act.

If someone can sign themselves into a facility, a family member or someone else is also asked to sign the admission paperwork. This ensures that the facility has someone to seek payment from for the services rendered to the patient. If this individual reads the paperwork, they will see that they are responsible for repayment after death of the patient or changes in placement.

I remember when I went through this process as the family member who signed the admissions paperwork. I received a $5,000.00 bill within the first few weeks for services before my family member got approved for Nursing Home Medicaid. I prayed that they would meet the spenddown for assistance. It took 60 to 90-days after applying for the benefits and working with the admission staff to get an approval. As a result, my family member was able to remain in the facility for the care needed due to her medical condition. She remained there until her death 1 1/2 years later. Within 30 to 45 days after her death, I received a balance for approximately $65,000.00 for the Medicaid benefits used to pay for her care.

I did not panic because I was familiar with the process being a medical social worker and it being my responsibility for after-care placements. I followed directions of who to call for assistance and there was no cost required from me. *The key was and will always be to follow directions and add to your support system.* Not doing this would have made me responsible for the majority of costs, and I would have been forced to take out a loan because I did not have the cash to pay the bills.

Next, if individuals have money in personal bank accounts at the time of placement or if they have rental property, the state or facility can also gain access to the funds to help with payment for care services. This means the loss of family and personal properties, money, assets, insurance payouts after death, etc.

Also, when one is admitted to some care facilities, they are allowed to keep a few dollars monthly ($50 to $75) for what is referred to as personal care need purchases. The cost for items such as in room cable, TVs, clocks, radios, phone service, clothing, and hair care

are usually not covered by insurances. So, if someone does not have extra support, he or she will likely not have access to these items by their control.

Spousal Impoverishment

Inquiring about Spousal Impoverishment might be beneficial to married couples when placements are required because of health changes. This is a benefit that if someone is legally married and can prove that their spouse's income is needed to help them with their immediate living expenses, the individual can possibly keep a percentage of the spouse's income instead of it all going to the facility to pay for the patient's care when the time is required.

This is a benefit like others that should be discussed before or at the time of admission so that after the insurance-approved stay, the income would remain with the spouse not in placement, if eligible.

No Insurance Coverage

If someone does not have insurance coverage to pay for outpatient or inpatient services, speak with admissions or financial assistance staff and ask if they have benefits that can help with costs. There might be programs, grants, or city and county funds to pay for services if the patient meets the criteria.

Understanding In and Out-Patient Network Insurance Providers

Before admission to facilities or setting up medical or mental health appointments, review your insurance provider's directory to learn the difference between in-network and out-of-network services and payments to providers. Several providers might accept the coverage that you have, but if you remain in-network versus going out-of-network, co-pays tend to be less, and insurance payments are more to the providers because they have contracts for services.

If there are services that providers out-of-network offer that in-network providers do not, let the insurance company know the area where you reside, and there might be a possibility that a payment contract can be developed so that the services can be accessed by the consumer without going out of the local area and without as much of an out-of-network cost.

There will be times when negotiations are not allowed for out-of-network services and the consumer will pay the full cost for choosing that provider. For example, my dentist is no longer in-network, and because I chose to keep services with him, I am responsible for covering the full cost of the bill at the time services are rendered. However, my insurance company agreed to reimburse me at a lower rate. Next, pay attention to annual benefit maximums because once they are reached during a calendar year, the consumer is usually responsible for 100% of bills for that service.

Bill Balances

Let insurance companies and providers know if you have more than one policy to pay for services. Rest assured that they will find out, and policies can be jeopardized. Another reason is because it will help the consumer better understand how coverage will be paid by each company. One policy will be considered the primary and the other secondary.

Keep in mind that each has a deductible that must be met before there are payouts to providers for certain services. Having multiple policies does not mean that there will be a 100% payout for all bills.

It is also advised to check with the insurance company's payouts to providers for services before they are rendered. Doing this is advantageous because one will be aware of costs of procedures, medications, or estimated costs which can help someone make informed decisions and planning. Write down questions and call the numbers provided by facilities and companies and speak with billing or other appropriate staff. It is my experience that if you have questions ready and are not trying to remember when speaking with representatives, answers are clearer. Afterall, you know what you need clarification regarding.

After questions are answered, call several times if additional clarification is needed. Next, ask if the facility can offer additional or any discounts to help lower the balance. For instance, there are facilities that have programs that might clear a portion of the bill balance if the person meets the financial or other eligibility criteria. There are also facilities that will give a discount that is given to insurance companies if balances are paid in full. I have gotten 5 to 10 percent discounts on balances just for asking. Keep in mind that the discount might not be honored if the bill cannot be paid in full. Consider paying the balance in full to avoid interest that might be added if the account is set up on a monthly payment plan. Paying monthly, adds to the balance making payments higher.

If the decision is to pay the bill in full, give some thought to the means available for accessing the funds to do this. Also, check interest rates. You might be able to secure a payment method that has a lower payment and interest on the balance compared to paying the amount that the provider quotes.

If someone is under-insured or has a bill balance that they cannot afford to pay in full, check with the facility and ask if they have a Financial Assistance Program. Some will have such assistance and others will not. This allows adjustments to bills based on eligibility. For some, this might mean a bill going from a balance to no balance at all, or percentages off which lowers the balance/s owed.

Lastly, become familiar with the Aged, Blind and Disabled Medicaid services offered through the Division of Family and Children Services (DFCS), the name in Georgia. Each benefit has eligibility criteria which must be met before assistance can be rendered.

Benefits in Georgia include the following:

- Institutionalized- requires a spenddown discussed in the placement section

- Qualified Medicare
  Beneficiaries (QMB) -helps
  with payment for Medicare
  coinsurance and deductibles

- Specified Low-Income
  Medicare Beneficiaries
  (SLMB)- assists with the
  monthly premium for
  Medicare Supplemental
  Medical Insurance Part B

- Adult Medically Needy- has
  no income maximum and
  allows individuals to use
  medical expenses to "spend

down" the difference between their income and the medically needy income level and other services available.

Again, each has eligibility requirements, and one should speak with appropriate individuals and ask questions.

Medical Equipment

If medical equipment is needed, a prescription or physician's order should be obtained for insurance assistance. Office staff will usually help with this process so that questions are answered most appropriately regarding the medical needs of a patient. If someone is in a facility, staff should assist because it is a part of the discharge planning process.

Please know that benefits differ on policies. For instance, if a walker or scooter is needed, the benefit might cover the full cost or a percentage if there is supporting medical documentation that the equipment might be beneficial for the individual's care or safety. However, if someone purchases one of the above items simply because they want it and there is no supporting documentation for its need, the individual will likely pay full cost with no reimbursement by an insurance company.

If equipment is approved, insurance companies tend to payout a larger amount to the provider, if the deductible is paid and the provider is in network. If the deductible is not paid, the out-of-pocket cost is higher until the deductible has been met. For instance, if a CPAP machine is needed and the deductible has not been met for the year, the patient will have a higher monthly rental cost compared to one whose deductible has been met for the same machine.

An insurance provider or medical staff will let the patient know what the out-of-pocket cost is to rent or pay for the equipment monthly. Yes, there are rental fees for some equipment if the patient's cost is not paid in full. Equipment is not owned until it is paid for, and not all equipment might be desired for ownership.

In some cases, equipment will be rented for the time that the patient needs it. From my working experience, I had many discussions with insurance companies regarding buying equipment versus renting it for long periods due to someone's medical diagnoses or the status of their condition. After all, insurance companies prefer to do business in cost effective ways and the patient benefits from not having extended financial costs.

When in-home equipment is required, someone from an equipment company might come to the home to complete an assessment which likely includes taking measurements before cost and delivery are finalized. For instance, doors and spaces might have to be measured and modifications made to home structures to accommodate the equipment. More often than not, if structural modifications are required, permission from the owner of the property must be obtained prior to the work being done. Otherwise, legal issues between the owner and renter might occur. If permission is not granted one might be forced to change his or her placement site.

Another way to obtain medical equipment is to reach out to community agencies and organizations and ask if they help with purchasing, installing, loaning, or building equipment for free or at reduced cost. I remember reaching out to a company at a time when a family needed a stairlift to get their loved one up and down steps in the home. The company had several donations from families no longer needing them in their homes. Because the equipment was used, it was sold for an affordable cost and the company discounted the installation cost for the family because of the circumstances. Because I was a part of the family's support system, I was instrumental in getting an agency to assign a licensed contractor to donate supplies and labor for additions. The contractor took care of the installation of a wheelchair ramp along with safety rails throughout the home. The company did not charge fees for services; they only asked for donations.

Victims Compensation Program

If someone's injuries, hospitalizations, or death is related to them being a victim of a crime, consider reaching out to the Criminal Justice Coordinating Council (the name in Georgia). To find out if the state of which you reside has a program, reach out to Victim Witness, local courts, and/or other related programs to inquire. This program helps innocent victims and/or their family members with financial costs resulting from various losses. For instance, the program aids with medical expenses, dental expenses, lost wages, funeral expenses, counseling expenses, crime scene sanitization expenses, etc. Benefit amounts vary, and there are forms, applications, and other documents required to meet eligibility.

Auto Loan Disability Insurance

If a life-changing event occurs while paying for a vehicle and payments are not made, repossession is likely to happen. Because of the above, consider purchasing auto loan disability insurance. This coverage makes car loan payments for an eligible period if one becomes ill or injured and cannot work under the terms in the agreement. This is an optional purchase that can be included in or with the car loan if available. Check with the lender and/or dealership about the above and eligibility. I cannot mention how many people purchased the coverage after being informed, experienced health challenges while paying for their vehicles, and did not stress about payments or repossessions. What they spent to purchase for a monthly premium was less than going to a movie and getting refreshments.

Home and Apartment Coverages

Stop stressing yourselves by avoiding spending money on what can destress you. It is amazing how people will spend money foolishly and hesitate to spend it on what can help them and their family live in a state of more comfort and peace. Storms, hurricanes, tornadoes, sicknesses, and illnesses happen all the time and impact families regardless of their socioeconomic status, who they know, or where they live.

If you own or are interested in buying a home, consider Mortgage Disability Coverage. This is a coverage that will help to pay the mortgage if the mortgage holder becomes sick or ill for a time specified in the policy. The mortgage provider is usually not the one that offers this coverage.

One must have a covered sickness or illness along with medical proof for the payments to be made. Funds are paid monthly to the policy holder and usually in the amount of the mortgage if the paperwork is up-to-date. Plainly speaking, if a person refinances a home, the policy holder or holders should inform the company holding the policy so the necessary adjustments will be made with premium payments. There is a payment waiting period specified on policies and medical proof must be provided on an ongoing basis to verify the illness or sickness. The company will let the policy-holder know if premiums are due during the time that they are disabled or unable to work.

Next, there are policy limits for payments. It is stated in one provider's information that payments will not exceed 12-months per approved sickness or illness. Rates for the coverage tend to be based on the monthly mortgage amount, the number of people on a policy, age, and other qualifying factors. One of my friends who took advantage of this additional coverage has a monthly payment of $60 for a mortgage that is $1,200 monthly. What a small amount to pay to secure a payment instead of repossession of a home?

This coverage was and remains a stress-reducer for those who purchased it after my sharing the information. People got sick, ill, and were not able to work while paying mortgages but did not stress about the payments or foreclosures.

Mortgage Life Protection Coverage

Mortgage Life Protection is a benefit that is also considered a stress-reducer. It gives one the relief of knowing that when they die, if their home is not paid in full, the family will be able to remain there without a mortgage payment.

In the past, Mortgage Disability Coverage could be purchased without Mortgage Life Protection, but when I called a few companies to verify if this could still be done, I was informed that both had to be purchased if the first was desired. This means there would be two premiums. Life Protection, however, can be purchased alone (1 premium) with some companies. Again, this might not be offered by the mortgage company. If asked about the coverages, some companies will gladly provide contact information where they can be purchased.

With regards to the protection, it will be in the amount of the mortgage loan. As it is being paid down, the policy value decreases. Meaning that if the mortgage loan amount was originally $250,000, after the mortgage is paid in full there is no longer a $250,000 insurance value or policy.

Instead of purchasing Mortgage Life Protection, some find it more advantageous to purchase a life insurance policy in the amount equal or with more value than the home cost or balance. If this can be done, this benefit will not decrease in value as the mortgage is being paid down or decreases. The value of the policy will be what was purchased if payments are consistent and other qualifications are met to allow such purchase. Again, timing is key.

Mortgage Protection Coverage

If you have a mortgage, consider Mortgage Protection Coverage as well. It is coverage that will pay the monthly mortgage if one is displaced from their home due to damage from fire, flood, windstorms, gas leakages, etc. for a specific period. Some coverage will pay the mortgage loan off up to the limit that is listed in the policy if the home is no longer livable. This is not insurance; it is coverage that works in addition to the insurance coverage on a home while it is being paid for.

The premium tends to be decided for purchasing this coverage by the monthly mortgage amount and the unpaid balance of the mortgage at the time of purchase. There are companies that also offer a one-time and/or ongoing monthly payment to help with living expenses up to the amount listed in the policy, until the policy-holder is able to live in the home again.

A few companies explained that their payout to assist with living expenses is $1,000 per incident, and payments on the mortgage start the next month after a claim is filed. Proof from the homeowner's insurance company must be verified and that the home is unlivable. There is also a time limit for the mortgage assistance, 1-year or less by one company. It was shared that if a home was not rebuildable or repairable, the mortgage would be paid off to the balance owed or up to the coverage limit. There is ongoing communication between the companies. This coverage has a limit on the payments for property, and benefits are in addition to whatever a homeowner coverage policy is or will provide.

I remember after flooding in a state years ago, a bank sent information about the coverage to those with balances over $100,000. They were willing to allow mortgage holders to add the monthly premiums for coverage with the mortgage payment and they accepted responsibility for sending the payments to the company. Keep in mind, that when disasters happen, it does not mean that a mortgage loan will be paid in full by an insurance company. The homeowner might have to pay the loan off and pay on a new or another loan for new property.

Homeowners Insurance Coverage

Homeowners insurance is required when there are mortgages, and it is also in the best interest for the homeowner to have it if they own property after the mortgage is paid in full. Claims are made when there is assistance needed for repairs and damages caused by floods, fires, roof leaks, pipes bursting, tree damage, hurricanes, tornadoes, and storms, if it is covered under the policy.

It is encouraged to read your policy to learn what is covered and what is not covered. It is also encouraged to confirm policy deductible amounts and limits per incident. There can be different deductibles on one policy.

I remember a relative who changed insurers thinking that cheaper would be better. This person had a policy with a company for over 15-years. He did not compare the policy that he had to the new policy purchased which he later regretted. When making a claim to the new insurer for repairs due to a tree falling on the house as well as hail and wind damages, he learned that there was a $1,000 deductible for some damage or incidents, and a $10,000 deductible for the others.

This individual learned that the policy purchased years ago had better coverages although it was more expensive than the newer one. He also learned that the older policy was no longer available for purchase or repurchase, so he had to keep the new policy. He ended up getting a loan to help with paying the deductible for the higher repair costs.

Also, assess if flood insurance is worth considering for additional coverage. The reason is because what is not in a flood area today might be tomorrow, and when water accesses property or homes, there are usually limits on basic policies that will not cover specific costs related to water and other damages as a flood policy would. This is also a policy that is not a high cost for what is covered when incidents occur. Put your shields and armors aside and ask informed questions to the appropriate experts for clarification.

Renter's Insurance

Everyone does not own a home and is not interested in being a homeowner. If you are renting, consider renters insurance. Homeowners tend to have coverage on their property to protect assets which usually does not cover the rentee's assets. Some renters offer coverage and will add it to the rent payment and others require proof of insurance purchase before the move-in-date.

This insurance is advantageous to all if an unfortunate incident occurs, and repairs must be made to the property or personal items of the rentee need to be replaced. This does not often have an expensive premium compared to the cost of what can be lost without the coverage. The cost of the insurance can be cheaper than what some pay for a restaurant meal.

Home Warranty and Repairs

I have been in many homes and heard about sicknesses and illnesses developed by individuals because they did not have working appliances or items. They were unable to keep medicines cool, keep themselves comfortable (heat and cool), there were pipe leaks, washers and dryers not working, stoves and microwaves not working, and electrical cords everywhere because of shortages in sockets, etc.

If you are a homeowner or thinking about becoming one, consider a home warranty. When buying a home, major appliance issues, air conditioning and heating problems, washer and dryer issues, electrical issues, garage operational issues, and plumbing problems, are at the repair expense of the homeowner. There is the thought that homeowner's insurance covers the above, but most will not unless it is stated as a covered expense under specific circumstances.

There are many companies that offer home warranties, and they can be purchased during the time one is paying a mortgage or after a home is purchased. Policies are offered at different costs, and they do not all have the same covered repairs. One company that I am familiar with offers different payment options. There are different deductibles that are paid at the time services are rendered by contractors for covered repairs, and they replace approved parts and items if they cannot be repaired at little to no additional cost outside of the deductible. Another company explained that policy owners must pay for covered repairs out-of-pocket, and they reimburse up to the limit specified in the policy for the approved repairs.

A warranty of such might not be needed, but unless you have access to hundreds and thousands of dollars when there are malfunctions or issues with appliances or different items, paying for a warranty and deductible is cheaper than service charges, item replacements, parts, getting loans to pay for costly items, and having to wait months and years to save for the purchase or repairs.

If you are renting, learn what renters' rights are and speak with the landlord sooner than later when repairs are needed. Make sure to read or have someone read the lease regarding the mentioned before you move in. Lastly, reach out as needed to appropriate individuals to help you advocate for your rights.

Bank Accounts

If you have a bank account, no matter the amount or how many, consider a Payable on Death (POD) beneficiary if the account is eligible. This is a bank account or accounts which allows the owner to designate one or more beneficiaries to receive the funds in the account when the owner dies. Beneficiaries can be an individual, group of individuals, non-profit, etc. Again, there are certain accounts eligible for PODs and others are not. This might keep money out of probate when the owner dies. Probate is the legal process of settling the property of the individual who has died. When someone dies, the funds in their account or accounts usually become part of their estate. But when a POD beneficiary is usually named, the funds can possibly pass directly to the named person, as determined by the state law or laws.

Per bank staff, after the death of the account owner, one notifies them, and they will work together to verify what is necessary for the payout by passing probate court for PODs. Beneficiaries for this account like others, can be changed whenever the owner desires for a change to be made. Being married or the children of someone at the time of their death does not mean that the money will be inherited by any of these persons. There are also state laws regarding if a beneficiary is under 21 years old.

The above should be discussed with appropriate banking staff as well as legal representatives so that whomever someone desires to inherit their monies are able to properly access it along with other things.

I recall so many times that such planning was not in place before someone's death and family's lost homes, assets, and became homeless because funds were not accessible when needed or people had to wait until probate was completed, which can take months to years to be settled.

Dr. Kendall Johnson

Payees

As lives change because of mental and physical disabilities, a payee or someone to serve as power of attorney over finances and other things might be considered. This person would be able to assist the disabled individual with paying rent, bills, buying groceries and/or help with other necessities. If appointed, the person should be trustworthy, dependable, honest, and have the welfare of the other person at heart. This can be done legally and/or according to where benefits are received from. For instance, someone might legally appoint a power of attorney over finances but with some Social Security funds a payee must be appointed by the person receiving the benefits. As I was told by Social Security staff, the legal power of attorney over finances is not recognized with some funds issued by them. Keep in mind, as situations change, the above can change as well.

There are agencies available in communities that are authorized to act as payees for those who are required or need to have such and do not personally select someone. To find out which agencies are authorized to do such can be done by inquiring with where the benefits are being received from and possibly Division of Family and Children Services (DFCS). Regardless of how the selection is made, hopefully there is someone willing to monitor to make sure that the disabled individual is not taken advantage of by the appointed person, agency, or others. If they are, report it to the appropriate authorities for a legal investigation or other actions to result. After all, this population is taken advantage of more often than not.

Ending

It is my hope that information in this book is meaningful and will help people understand why having multiple systems in their lives is beneficial. This is only helpful when people are willing to put the armors and shields away and ask appropriate questions to experts or those who possess the knowledge. This can be challenging, so it is advised to ask others to help you ask questions as needed. I found this to be advantageous because when people are emotionally upset or deeply impacted by things, they are guided by emotions, but the world operates from a business standpoint. Sometimes, when businesses, companies, or people see and hear the vulnerability of a person, they are taken advantage of. In such cases, help is not rendered in the same manner that one would get who has a different approach or asks specific questions.

Keep in mind, everyone will receive a phone call, knock at the door, or a text message that will change your life in some manner. Knowing about resources can help reduce stressors temporarily or permanently.

About the Author

Dr. Kendall Johnson is CEO and Executive Director of Success for Families and Children Enterprises and Success for Children and Families, Inc. She is a part-time professor of social work at two universities, works in collaboration with local and worldwide courts and judicial systems, serves on several boards of directors, and worked in corrections. Dr. Johnson provides crisis and grief counseling on all levels, works with domestic violence cases, provides substance abuse services, facilitates parenting classes, and has experience working with teen pregnancy. She works nationally in collaboration with the Division of Family and Children Services and worked as a medical social worker several years. Dr. Kendall Johnson also served as an administrator at a children's center and multiple mental health facilities.

Dr. Johnson has over 40-years of experience in the profession of social work. She possesses a Doctorate of Education (Ed.D), a Master of Social Work, and Bachelor Social Work Degrees. She is licensed by the state of Georgia and in the state of Rhode Island to practice social work. The author is a National Certified Domestic Violence Counselor (CDVC), State of Georgia Approved Domestic Violence

Facilitator, Nationally Certified Custody Evaluator, Nationally Certified Parenting Coordinator, Certified Mental Health First Responder, and an Employee Assistance Program provider for several companies. She possesses a Master Addiction Certification (MAC), is EMDR Therapy Trained, a Substance Abuse Professional (SAP), and possesses several additional national certificates and certifications.